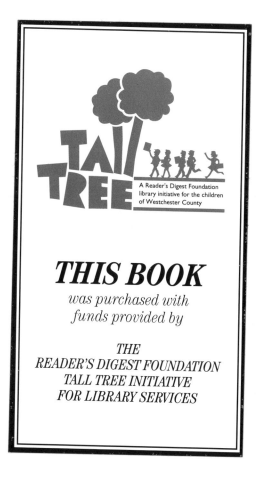

A Reader's Digest Foundation
library initiative for the children
of Westchester County

THIS BOOK

was purchased with
funds provided by

THE
READER'S DIGEST FOUNDATION
TALL TREE INITIATIVE
FOR LIBRARY SERVICES

GREG MADDUX
ACE!

GREG MADDUX
ACE!

John A. Torres

Lerner Publications Company • Minneapolis

For Jackie, my little one, who fills my heart with incredible joy; to Mom and Dad for teaching me to love the beauty of sports

This book is available in two editions:
Library binding by Lerner Publications Company
Soft cover by First Avenue Editions
241 First Avenue North, Minneapolis, Minnesota 55401

Library of Congress Cataloging-in-Publication Data

Torres, John Albert.
    Greg Maddux, ace! / John A. Torres.
      p.   cm.
    Includes bibliographical references (p.) and index.
    Summary: A biography of the ace pitcher who won the Cy Young award
four times and who currently plays for the Atlanta Braves.
    ISBN 0–8225–3650–1 (hardcover: alk. paper). — ISBN 0–8225–9768–3 (pbk.: alk. paper)
    1. Maddux, Greg, 1966– —Juvenile literature. 2. Baseball
players—United States—Biography—Juvenile literature. 3. Pitchers
(Baseball)—United States—Biography—Juvenile literature.
[1. Maddux, Greg, 1966– . 2. Baseball players.] I. Title.
GV865.N319T65 1997
796.357'092—dc21
[B]   97–8102

Manufactured in the United States of America
1 2 3 4 5 6 – JR – 02 01 0 0 99 98 97

Contents

Hitters know that batting against Greg is a tough job.

A Dominating Pitcher

The stadium was packed with frenzied fans hoping that Atlanta's third trip to the World Series would finally be the charm. The Atlanta Braves boasted baseball's most talented pitching staff. The only obstacle standing in their way was a hard-hitting Cleveland Indians lineup.

When Atlanta's ace starting pitcher, Greg Maddux, took the mound in the 1995 World Series opener, most of the Cleveland Indians could not believe their eyes. They had heard many things about the National League's most dominating pitcher, but they never expected this.

The word "dominating" usually stirs up images of size, power, and speed. Dominating athletes are usually bigger, stronger, and faster than the average player. However, as Greg Maddux warmed up to face Cleveland, it was obvious that the National League's

7

most dominating righthanded pitcher was the exact opposite of these images. After all, Greg is less than 6 feet tall, weighs no more than 180 pounds, and rarely throws a fastball faster than 85 miles an hour. Yet, he has become baseball's best pitcher, baffling National League batters for the better part of eight seasons and certainly for the last four.

The Cleveland Indians did not seem to be intimidated by Greg in the first inning of the World Series. Cleveland leadoff hitter Kenny Lofton chopped a harmless grounder to shortstop. But Rafael Belliard booted the easy grounder, allowing the speedy Lofton to reach base. Lofton proceeded to easily steal second base and then third base. Now Cleveland had a man on third with no one out and its big guns coming to the plate.

Greg did not change his style once, nor did he flinch at the pressure of the situation. Some pitchers would be tight and tend to overthrow in a situation like that, but not Greg.

Like a surgeon, he **painted the corners,** precisely putting the ball where he wanted it. He retired the next three All-Star batters—Carlos Baerga, Eddie Murray, and Albert Belle—and the ball never left the infield. Lofton scored on a groundout, but that was the only run Cleveland could muster. Greg held baseball's best hitting team to just two hits as the Braves took the opener of the Series.

Cleveland's Eddie Murray tells Greg not to throw the ball
so far inside during their 1995 World Series matchup.

Dale Murphy, former Braves All-Star outfielder and two-time Most Valuable Player, praised Greg after the game. "What can you say about him?" asked Murphy. "He's simply one of a kind, a throwback to the pitchers of 50 years ago. What makes him so great is that he just doesn't make mistakes. A lot of pitchers don't know what hitters don't like. Unpredictability is Greg's greatest asset. He's got so many different pitches, that if you're a hitter, you never know what's coming from him."

While Greg is an ace pitcher and a one-of-a-kind talent, many fans wouldn't recognize him on the street. Greg wears small round spectacles when he's not pitching, and doesn't look like a star athlete. He doesn't like to brag about his pitching, and he refuses to do commercials. "I'll be out with him," says Atlanta pitcher John Smoltz, "and people will recognize me. Greg can walk right through a crowd of people."

With his modest style, slight frame, and average fastball, Greg has amassed Hall of Fame credentials. His statistics compare only with those of the great Walter Johnson, dubbed the "The Big Train," who overpowered hitters in the early 1900s. Johnson won 20 or more games a season for 10 straight seasons. Johnson won a whopping 36 games one year, and another year he struck out 313 batters. From 1992 to 1995, Greg led the major leagues in wins, innings pitched, and **earned run average (ERA).**

Walter Johnson struck out 3,508 batters during his 21-year career, from 1907 to 1927. He was 6 feet tall and weighed about 200 pounds, but people called him "The Big Train" because he was always on track.

An ERA is a good measure of a pitcher's talent. It indicates how many runs a pitcher allows the opposing team per every nine innings pitched. Without a blistering fastball or sharp breaking **curveball,** Greg often leaves batters bewildered.

"I think he's gotten even better from when I faced him a few years ago," said Braves catcher Charlie O'Brien, who batted against Greg as a New York Met.

Greg wears glasses when he's practicing or not playing.

"I've never seen so many guys leaving the plate saying, 'How did he do that?' "

How he does it is a simple procedure, after some research and hard work. Greg has flawless control, placing most pitches exactly where he wants to, using varying degrees of speed. He is able to throw many types of pitches: fastball, **cut fastball,** curveball, **slider,** and an amazing **changeup.** Not many pitchers are able to throw five kinds of pitches. Although he doesn't have one specific pitch that he uses to get a batter out, Greg has great command of all five types of pitches.

What makes Greg so good is that he is able to throw any one of his pitches for a strike at any time. A hitter can never just sit back and expect a certain pitch in a certain location. Even though Greg does strike out a lot of hitters, he is known as a ground ball pitcher. This means that he usually keeps his pitches low in the strike zone, which forces the batter to hit the ball on the ground. A power pitcher, or strikeout pitcher, usually relies on a high-rising fastball that results in a lot of strikeouts and fly balls. One great power pitcher, Nolan Ryan, threw the ball 100 miles an hour and also threw a tantalizing curveball. Yet, even though Ryan threw much harder, he didn't always throw the ball where he wanted to and was never able to put together a string of successful seasons like Greg's.

By studying opposing hitters when he's not pitching, Greg learns their habits.

"I could probably throw a lot harder if I wanted to," Greg says, "but I think it is more important to locate better. Young pitchers tend to throw harder when they are in a jam. I just try to move the ball around a little bit more."

Most successful pitchers keep charts and books on opposing hitters to help them remember what certain hitters like and dislike. The average pitcher will keep track of the pitches and their locations that he used to get a batter out and which pitches a batter was able to hit hard. For example, every pitcher knows that slugger Darryl Strawberry is a good low-ball hitter. Knowing that, most pitchers try to pitch the ball high or outside to him.

Greg also knows exactly what and where he threw to a batter during their last encounter. Greg keeps all this information in his charts, although he probably wouldn't have to because he has an amazing memory for hitters. He studies hitters' habits, stances, and styles. Greg's idea is to educate himself about his opponent and throw the ball where *Greg* wants it to go.

"He's able to notice things in the course of a game that no one else can," says star Braves pitcher Tom Glavine. "He notices the way a hitter may open up a little, move up in the box, change his stance. I've tried to be aware of that stuff—I really have. I don't know how he does it."

Greg watches batting practice with Tom Glavine.

Greg grew up playing baseball in Las Vegas and dreaming of playing in the big leagues.

Mike's Little Brother

Gregory Alan Maddux was born on April 14, 1966, in the town of San Angelo, Texas. But Greg really does not consider himself to be a Texan. His father, David, was in the United States Air Force. He and Greg's mother, Linda, had to move the family every time Greg's father was transferred. Greg, his older sister, Terri, and his older brother, Mike, received an international education by growing up in Texas, California, North Dakota, Ohio, Alaska, Taiwan, Spain, and Nevada.

Greg's brother and father both loved sports. By the time Greg was six years old, he was also active in baseball and basketball. Greg would wait in the back-yard every day at 3:30 for his dad to get home from work at the Air Force base in Madrid, Spain. The two would immediately put on their baseball gloves and play catch. They started out just playing catch. Soon, six-year-old Greg was learning how to wind up like a pitcher and step toward his father, who would crouch down like a catcher. Greg's dad was amazed at his son's natural pitching motion.

There weren't many children Greg's age at the Air Force bases, so he often played with Mike and his friends, who were about five years older. Greg didn't realize it at the time, but playing with the older boys really helped him improve his baseball skills.

"I would always go and play ball and Greg would always tag along," says Mike. "He was 4½ years younger than the other kids, so there was a tremendous physical difference. But I always made him my first-round draft pick. Besides, he was better than a lot of guys my age."

Mike never minded his little brother's admiration. Mike wore his baseball cap backwards, so Greg did too. Mike constantly pounded his fist into his glove, so Greg did too. Mike used to spit, making believe he was chewing tobacco, so Greg did too. "He played with me and my friends up until I went to college," Mike says. "He was never a standout in our games. But he was so far ahead of guys his own age."

By the time Greg played against kids his own age, he was dominating the games. "Greg benefited greatly by competing with the older boys," his father says. "He was never intimidated by the age difference. That amazed me."

Greg was lucky to have parents who were encouraging and supportive. Greg and Mike were allowed to stay out late, as long as they were playing baseball. The baseball field became a home base for a family that was forced to move to new surroundings every few years. The one constant, no matter where they moved, was that every place had a baseball field.

"In Spain, we didn't have television so we had to create our own fun," Greg said. "We didn't do anything that cost money. We had a ball, a glove, and a bat, and entertained ourselves. Luckily, there was no Nintendo. My parents didn't mind us playing baseball. We were good kids, and as long as you're on a baseball field, you can't get into trouble."

After Greg's father retired from the Air Force, the Maddux family moved to Las Vegas, Nevada. Greg was 10 years old and Mike had just turned 15. Their father got a job as a card dealer at a Las Vegas casino, where he still works. Soon, a retired major league scout named Ralph Medar began coaching Mike. Medar offered informal instruction to some of Las Vegas's best young players. As usual, Greg would tag along with Mike to the Sunday practices.

After a month or so, David Maddux talked Medar into letting Greg play with the much older kids. Medar was skeptical, especially because Greg was so much smaller than the rest of the players. But Greg quickly impressed the coach.

By the time Greg played for his high school team, he was way ahead of other players his age.

"I don't know where this boy got those **pitching mechanics**," Medar said, "but let me tell you this: don't let anyone change those mechanics—he's going to be something."

Medar did not want Greg to throw curveballs or sliders because he was so young. Many young kids ruin their arms and their motions by throwing curve-balls. Throwing a curveball puts tremendous strain on a pitcher's elbow. Most Little League coaches discourage their pitchers from throwing curves because their arms are still developing. Even in the major leagues, a pitcher will not throw a curveball until his arm is thoroughly warmed up and loose. Instead of a curveball, Medar taught Greg to throw a changeup.

"Down the line, a good changeup is harder to hit than any other pitch," Medar said. Medar also showed Greg how to lower his arm and throw the ball at a three-quarters position. With a three-quarters motion, Greg's arm was parallel to his ear, instead of high above his ear, as it is when he throws straight over the top.

Medar also told Greg to switch from a four-seam fastball to a two-seamer. There are many different ways to grip and throw a baseball. The number of fingers, the seams that are used, and the amount of strength used to hold and throw a baseball all help determine what the ball will do. Some balls will sink or rise mainly because of the grip and speed with which they are thrown. Other pitches will tail away from a hitter, while still others dive sharply toward the batter.

When Greg switched from holding the ball with two fingers across two seams to two fingers down two seams, the results were spectacular. His fastball moved furiously all over the place. Most of the time, Greg's fastball slowly tailed away from a righthanded hitter.

Greg was so far ahead of kids his own age that he dominated his Little League. When he was 12 years old, Greg's Little League coach refused to have him pitch in the championship game because he said it was not fair to the opposing team. The other teams in the league could barely make any contact against Greg. Since Greg was such a good hitter, he still got a chance to play in the game, and his team won the championship.

Greg met his future wife, Kathy, at Valley High School in Las Vegas. Greg was an above-average student, but he says he could have worked harder and gotten better grades. He spent his free time playing sports and working part-time at the local Wendy's Restaurant. Greg graduated from Valley High in 1984.

Although he was only 5 feet, 11 inches tall and weighed all of 150 pounds, he was considered a potential first-round draft pick in the Major League Baseball amateur draft that June. In the amateur baseball draft, teams take turns picking the best college and high school players in the country. The team with the worst record the previous year picks first. Each team offers the players it has chosen a contract to play in its organization. If a player signs with a professional team, that player can't play high school or college baseball any more.

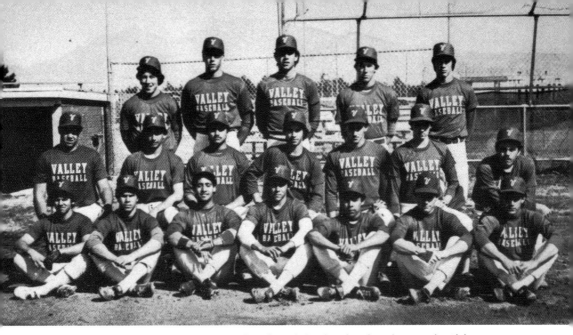

Mike is the player on the far right in the back row in this photo of his high school team.

Scott Boras, a baseball agent, advised Greg to skip the draft and go to college. Greg had already signed a **letter of intent** to play for the University of Arizona, one of the best college baseball programs in the country. But Greg was curious to know when he might be chosen in the draft, so he entered it. The Chicago Cubs drafted him in the second round and offered him an $85,000 bonus. He could not resist the offer and signed his first professional contract.

Greg's brother had been drafted by the Philadelphia Phillies in the 1982 draft. Mike was playing for one of the Phillies' minor league teams. Pitching in the major leagues was a dream Greg and Mike had always shared. Greg could hardly wait to get started!

Greg played for four minor league teams.

Becoming a Big Leaguer

When Greg signed his contract, he made himself a promise. He would not touch the $85,000 bonus until he made it to the major leagues. He would save the money for college, in case he did not make it to the big leagues. His father was very proud that Greg had been drafted. Some scouts had admitted to Greg's dad that they thought Greg was too small to be drafted. But now, both Maddux boys were playing professional baseball.

Every Major League Baseball team has a farm system, or group of minor league teams. In the minor leagues, the lowest level is rookie league, then Class A, Class AA, and Class AAA. Class AAA teams are just one step below the major leagues.

After being drafted, Greg reported to the Cubs' rookie league team in Pikeville, Illinois. He posted an impressive 6–2 record with a 2.63 ERA. In 1985, Greg was promoted to the Class A team in Peoria, Illinois. There, Greg won 13 games and had an ERA of 3.19.

The following year, Greg was sent to the Class AA team in Pittsfield, Massachusetts. There, Greg met major league pitching coach and former pitcher Dick Pole. Pole was the Pittsfield pitching coach. Since Greg's mechanics were already spectacular, Pole helped him with his **offspeed pitching.** Pole and Greg came up with the idea of moving Greg's thumb from underneath the ball to the side when he threw a changeup. That made Greg's changeup even harder to hit.

Even though Greg had posted winning records at every level, he still had doubts about his abilities. Pole showed Greg how to mix up his pitches. And most importantly, Pole helped Greg gain confidence in himself and all his pitches.

Midway through the season, Greg was promoted once again. This time he went to Chicago's Class AAA club in Des Moines, Iowa. Meanwhile, Greg's brother, Mike, had become a starting pitcher for the Philadelphia Phillies that summer.

Greg's hard work and great mechanics paid off quickly. He was called up to the Chicago Cubs in September 1986. In September, major league teams can add as many as 15 players to their roster, going from 25 to 40 players. Many teams call up their promising minor leaguers to give them a taste of the big leagues.

At Pittsfield, Greg learned to pitch at the major league level.

When Greg first reported to the Cubs, one of the coaches introduced him to the team's manager, Gene Michael. "I was standing in front of the dugout with one of my coaches—John Vokovich," Michael recalls. "He says to me, 'Aren't you going to say hello to your new pitcher?' I said, 'Where is he?' Vukovich points into the dugout at Greg. I said, 'That's the batboy' and he says, 'That's your new pitcher.' I will never forget that."

Greg pitched six times that fall, posting a 2–4 record with a very high earned run average of 5.52.

But his drive to win made a huge impression on the Cubs and their fans. One game, the Cubs sent him in as a **pinch runner.** He tried to score from second base on a single. There was a play at the plate, and Greg crashed into San Diego Padre catcher Benito Santiago, knocking the ball loose.

"The ball **short-hopped** Benito, so he was on his heels," Greg says. "I hate to think what would have happened if he had braced himself."

That play showed Chicago what kind of player Greg could be. Most pitchers would never put themselves at risk of an arm injury by diving into a catcher. Most would have stopped at third base.

That September, Greg got to pitch against his big brother. They became the first two brothers to pitch against each other since Joe and Phil Niekro did on September 13, 1982. The Maddux brothers were the first two rookie brothers to face each other. Their friendly rivalry intensified when Mike grounded a single to leftfield against Greg. When Greg came to bat the next inning, he was determined to get a hit.

"I singled to left too," Greg says with a laugh. "I had to get a hit or I would have had to hear about his all winter."

Despite his high ERA, Greg showed enough promise that fall to persuade the Cubs to put him on their opening day roster for 1987. Greg was the youngest player in the National League, and the season was sure to be a learning experience for him. He was named a starting pitcher at the age of 21. Like most young pitchers during their first season, Greg gave up a lot of hard hits.

Greg's brother, Mike, has pitched for several major league teams, including the Phillies, Mets, and Dodgers.

Greg first pitched for the big-league Cubs in 1986, but 1988 was his first full season as a major leaguer.

By July 24, Greg had a 6–8 record, but then he lost six consecutive games. His earned run average soared to more than five runs a game. He was sent back down to the minor leagues.

Greg was a little tense on the mound. He seemed to be rushing through his pitching motion. Playing for the Des Moines team, Greg worked hard on his mechanics. He won three straight starts for the Class AAA team. The Cubs called him back up in September when the rosters were expanded, but he did not win another game that season.

Greg finished his rookie season with a 6–14 record and a 5.61 ERA. He started 27 games, more than any other National League rookie pitcher. (A pitcher doesn't get credit for a win unless he pitches at least five innings. If a pitcher isn't credited with a win or a loss in a game in which he pitches, he's credited with a no-decision.) Greg also lost more games than any other rookie in the majors. He wasn't sure whether he would start the next season in the major or the minor leagues.

In the offseason, Greg married Kathy, his high school sweetheart. They bought a home in Las Vegas. They spent most of their free time playing cards or watching rented movies. "That's one of the things I liked about Greg from the beginning," Kathy says. "We'd both rather rent a movie than go out. We call ourselves Siskel and Ebert."

Greg and his wife, Kathy, met when they were in high school. Although Greg has become rich and famous, they still enjoy quiet times at home and playing games.

Greg also worked with Pole that winter. Greg pitched for Pole on a winter league team in Venezuela. Pole helped boost Greg's confidence. Greg had been relying on his fastball too much. Hitters were ready for it. Pole reminded Greg to mix up his pitches and to use his curveball or changeup in key situations.

When Greg arrived at spring training the next season, he figured he had only a 50-50 chance of making the team. The Cubs were not counting on him either. During the offseason, Chicago had traded for two starting pitchers, Al Nipper and Calvin Schiraldi. The two newcomers were slated to join Rick Sutcliffe, Jamie Moyer, and Les Lancaster to form a pretty good pitching staff.

"I wasn't one of the 24 guys," said Greg. "Common sense said that there was no place for me." But Greg made the Cubs officials change their plans. He had a terrific spring training. He was also lucky that the Cubs' new manager, Don Zimmer, watched him carefully. "He was 6–14 last year and I'm the new manager," Zimmer said. "What if he goes into spring training and is horrible? It turns out that he came in here and was the best pitcher on our club."

Greg overwhelmed National League hitters for the first half of the 1988 season. He pitched an outstanding streak of 26⅔ scoreless innings in May. In June, he was named the National League pitcher of the month after going 5–0 with a 2.22 ERA. And by the All-Star break in July, Greg had posted an incredible 15–3 record.

But for the second straight year, Greg suffered through a difficult second half of the season. Greg had never pitched so many innings in one season, and his coaches felt his arm may have become tired. Since he had pitched during the winter in Venezuela, Greg had never really rested his arm. He went just 3–5 in the second half, but finished with an 18–8 record.

Greg soon became known to his teammates and to fans as "Mad Dog," a nickname that he earned in Las Vegas. "The Mad Dog nickname is kind of a joke," Greg explains. "It is something that has been with me since high school because of my last name." Most of Greg's friends teased him because he was a mild-mannered person who rarely shows emotion. They thought that giving him a wild name was funny.

Greg's major league career was taking off at a fast pace. But instead of laying back and enjoying his success, Greg began to work even harder. He began studying films and videotapes of opposing hitters. By doing this, he could pick up any habits or traits that the hitter might have. He also began keeping very detailed notebooks and charts on how certain hitters had performed against him and on which pitches had proved most successful.

Most pitchers usually keep a chart or book on how teams hit against them. But Greg wanted more information than other pitchers did. He began recording how every hitter had done against him at every **count.**

Greg's dedication and conditioning have helped him maintain top form throughout his career.

He noticed who swung on the first pitch, who dug in with two strikes, who looked for a curveball with a full count, or who always waited for a fastball. Now that he was enjoying life in the major leagues, Greg didn't want to be average—he wanted to be the best.

By 1989, Greg was the Chicago Cubs' ace pitcher.

Great Expectations

Greg had gone from rookie to ace in just two short years. Going into the 1989 season, there would be a lot more pressure on the young pitcher. People expected Greg Maddux to be a winning pitcher. He did not disappoint them. Greg was soon dominating opponents for the second consecutive season. It wasn't long before he was recognized as a master on the pitcher's mound.

"He has shown a real ability to win close games," said former Montreal Expos manager Buck Rodgers. Whitey Herzog, a longtime manager and superb judge of talent, was impressed too. He was managing the St. Louis Cardinals at the time. "That kid is a very tough pitcher," Herzog said. "He knows what he is doing. He's going to win a lot of games."

The upstart Cubs soon found themselves in first place in the National League East Division, thanks mostly to their strong pitching. Greg finished the season with a 19–12 record and an outstanding earned run average of 2.95. The highlight of his season, however, was when he pitched the Cubs' title-clinching game on September 26. Chicago was going to the playoffs!

Greg made two starts against the West Division champion San Francisco Giants in the National League Championship Series. But his normally incredible control disappeared. He did not have very good command of his pitches and was hit hard. Greg allowed 11 runs in only 7½ innings to the powerhouse Giants, who had sluggers Kevin Mitchell, Will Clark, and Matt Williams in their lineup. Greg was 0–1 in the championship series with a loss and a no-decision. San Francisco won the series, four games to one.

The next season, 1990, was a tough one for Greg and for the Cubs. Greg got off to a fast start by going 4–1 in April with an almost unhittable ERA of 1.95. But then he lost eight straight decisions in 13 games.

Former mentor Dick Pole had left the Cubs before the season started. He was coaching for the Giants so he couldn't help Greg. During this difficult time, veteran Cubs pitcher Rick Sutcliffe encouraged Greg. Sutcliffe told Greg to just keep working hard, and he assured Greg that he would win again. Greg worked on keeping his fastball down in the strike zone, and soon he began winning again.

Greg struggled during the 1990 season, but won 15 games.

Sutcliffe couldn't explain the sudden turnabout in Greg's play. "Any pitcher depends on so many people," Sutcliffe said. "We [pitchers] need a lot of help offensively and defensively. One good play, one hit in the clutch, can change a game and change a losing streak. Now things are going Greg's way."

Greg finished the season with 15 wins and a respectable ERA of 3.46. He was among the National League leaders in several pitching categories. He also won a Gold Glove award by leading all pitchers with 94 total fielding chances without making an error. A Gold Glove is awarded to the best fielder at each position.

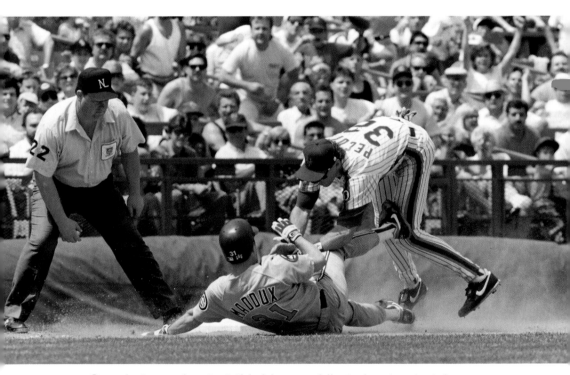

Greg is tagged out at third base while trying to stretch a double into a triple. Greg has 17 doubles as a major leaguer, but he has never hit a triple.

Greg was an established star pitcher. Most teams prepared to face him with a little more effort than they did other pitchers. This made Greg work even harder in his preparation. He watched more and more tapes of opposing hitters to try to gain an edge.

"I watch tapes of hitters all the time," Greg says. "When you go into a game with a certain plan and you execute it and it works, you walk away feeling like you've won even if you didn't win the game. Stuff like that is what pitching is all about. Pitching is the art of messing up a hitter's timing, of outguessing the hitter."

Greg won 15 games again in 1991. He also led the league with 37 starts and 263 innings pitched. He walked just 66 batters and struck out 198. Greg also won his second Gold Glove award.

Greg blew away the National League in 1992, winning 20 games with an ERA of only 2.11. He walked only 70 and struck out 199. He was 10–8 at the All-Star break and was named to the All-Star team.

Greg felt funny about pitching in the All-Star Game. "A hitter will get about 600 **at bats** over a year," Greg said. "He may see me only six or seven times out of those 600. I'm not going to do anything or say anything that makes him remember me." Greg also did not want any opposing hitters to be on the field behind him when he pitched in the All-Star Game. He was worried that they might pick up something that would help them hit his pitches. Greg did

end up attending the All-Star Game. If a player refused to go to an All-Star Game, baseball officials
would probably never invite that player again.

After the All-Star break, Greg went 10–3 with a
1.93 ERA for the second half of the season. He won
his third consecutive Gold Glove award. Greg also
was the clear winner of the National League's Cy
Young Award. The award, named after one of the
greatest pitchers who ever lived, is given every year
to the best pitcher in each league.

Cy Young won 511
games in 22 seasons,
from 1890 to 1911.
In five of those sea-
sons, he won 32
games or more.

Greg was thrilled to be named the Cy Young Award winner after his 1992 season.

Another reason Greg had gone to the All-Star Game was his competitive nature. He is even competitive at home with his wife. They love to play cards and Nintendo. Greg usually wins. He will challenge anyone, anytime. "I lost 26 consecutive games of Nintendo to him," says his agent, Scott Boras, "and then I watched him answer everything on *Jeopardy*." Kathy, Greg's wife, doesn't mind losing. "I let him win," she says, "because he can't stand to lose."

Besides playing Nintendo, cards, and watching videos, Greg loves to play golf. He is a good golfer, although his friends and teammates claim that he is lucky at the game too.

The following winter, Greg's contract with the Cubs ran out and he became a **free agent.** Greg was interested in staying with the Cubs, but he was also curious to see what other teams would offer. Many teams offered him good deals but he finally chose the National League's powerful Atlanta Braves.

The New York Yankees of the American League had offered him about $6 million more to play for them, but Greg did not want to change leagues and have to get to know all new hitters. He also did not like the pressure of being a team's star pitcher.

Atlanta already had a pitching staff of All-Stars. Greg was to join Tom Glavine, John Smoltz, and Steve Avery. Glavine had recently won a Cy Young Award. Smoltz and Avery were considered to be two of the best young pitchers in the game.

There was yet another reason Greg signed with the Braves. Atlanta had many talented players and was very close to winning a World Series. The Cubs and the Yankees still needed more good players. "I set out with three goals in the big leagues," Greg said. "Win 20 games, which I've done. Make $1 million, which I've done. And pitch in a World Series, which is still missing. Pitching in a World Series looks like a lot of fun—can't buy that." Greg set off to Atlanta to pursue his final dream: a World Series.

The Atlanta Braves were happy to have Greg join their already impressive pitching staff in 1993.

Playing in the World Series was Greg's goal, and he thought joining the Braves would help achieve it.

Mission Accomplished

Greg joined an Atlanta Braves team that had very high expectations going into the 1993 season. After all, the Braves had just lost their second consecutive World Series. They had lost in 1991 to the Minnesota Twins in seven games. Then in 1992, Atlanta lost to the Toronto Blue Jays in six games. The addition of one of the game's best pitchers to an already great pitching staff was expected to take them to the championship.

Greg pitched very well for the first half of the season but did not get the results he wanted. He posted a great 2.83 ERA but was only 8–8. "The most important statistic is games won," Greg said, expressing unhappiness with his record. "That's it."

In the second half of the season, Greg went 12–2 with an awesome earned run average of 1.79. He finished the season with a 20–10 record. He struck out 197 batters and walked only 52. His pitching helped the Braves clinch their third consecutive National League West championship. Greg won his first start of the playoffs against the Philadelphia Phillies but lost Game 6. The Phillies clinched the National League pennant with a 6–3 victory in that game. Greg's dream of pitching in a World Series would have to wait.

Greg was awarded his second consecutive Cy Young Award, joining Hall of Fame pitcher Sandy Koufax as the only National Leaguers ever to win back-to-back awards. Koufax was the most dominating lefthander of the 1960s. Pitching for the Los Angeles Dodgers, Koufax led the National League in ERA for five consecutive seasons. He won the Cy Young Award and was named the league's Most Valuable Player in 1963, when he posted a 25–5 record.

"You change teams and you want to make a good first impression," said Greg, who became the first pitcher to win the award in consecutive seasons with different teams. "I feel like I've done that. I really didn't change anything in the way I pitched. I pretty much tried to do the same things that have always worked in the past."

In 1994, Greg got off to a blazing start and had a 10–4 record by the All-Star break. Greg was named the starting pitcher for the National League in the All-Star Game. Although he did not really want to be in the game, Greg pitched for the first three innings.

Greg's new pitching teammates with the Atlanta Braves were: from left, Tom Glavine, Greg, Pete Smith, John Smoltz, and Steve Avery.

He allowed one run and struck out two. The National League won the game 8–7 in 10 innings.

After the break, Greg won five of his next six decisions with a terrific ERA of 0.87. He was not even allowing one run for every nine innings pitched! But by mid-August, negotiations between the Major League Baseball owners and the players were at a standstill. The two sides had been working to reach an agreement about how much money players would be paid.

The 1994 baseball season was cut short when the players went on strike. The strike delayed the start of the
1995 season, but play finally resumed.

They weren't able to agree, and on August 12, the
baseball players went on strike. The season was over.
No playoffs. No World Series. Greg's dream of playing in the World Series was put on hold again.

Postseason awards were given out, and Greg was given his third consecutive Cy Young Award. He did not mind winning it during a strike-shortened season. "I can certainly see people's complaints," he said. "It's like a rain-shortened game. It doesn't sour the award for me personally, but it was very frustrating. It's not just because of the year I was having, but because when I signed with Atlanta, one of my goals was to get into the World Series."

When the owners and players agreed on salary terms, the 1995 season began. The Braves were again the clear-cut favorite to win the World Series. The two-time defending champion Blue Jays had gotten older, and some of their players had left the team. The Braves had gone to the World Series or playoffs for three straight seasons. Were they ready to win it all? They had a pitching staff that included the previous four National League Cy Young Award winners. Tom Glavine had won the award in 1991, and Greg had won the next three.

Greg led the Braves in 1995 with an amazing 19–2 record and a 1.63 ERA. He became the first major leaguer since Hall of Famer Walter Johnson to post an ERA of under 1.80 in back-to-back seasons. He won his sixth straight Gold Glove, was the first pitcher ever to win the Associated Press Player of the Year award, and, of course, he became the first pitcher to ever win four consecutive Cy Young Awards.

In the 1995 playoffs, the Braves disposed of the hard-hitting Colorado Rockies, three games to one. Then Atlanta swept the Cincinnati Reds, four games to none. The Braves' starting pitchers—Greg, Smoltz, Glavine, and Avery—held the Reds to just four runs in 28 innings for the Series. This was especially remarkable because the Reds had been second in the league in scoring during the regular season. Atlanta's pitchers also held the Reds without a single home run, and Cincinnati had led the league in home runs that year. By the time the Braves pitchers faced the powerful Cleveland Indians, the Braves were confident that no one would be able to beat them.

Cleveland came to Atlanta with a monster hitting lineup. The Indians had hit 159 home runs, and boasted seven .300 hitters in their lineup. A .300 hitter is a hitter who gets a hit at least 3 out of every 10 times at bat.

Greg started the first game against Cleveland. He was a little nervous, but he overcame his jitters to dispose of the Indians on just 95 pitches—63 strikes!

Cleveland's manager, Mike Hargrove, needed just one word to describe Greg's performance. "Dominating," Hargrove said, frowning. "Dominating." After the game, Greg, modest as usual, said that "tonight was fun." Atlanta pitching coach Leo Mazzone was more enthusiastic: "I think you are seeing one of the greatest pitchers of all time."

Although pitchers aren't expected to be great hitters, Greg has 140 hits and 2 home runs as a major leaguer!

Greg pitched well in Game 5, his next start of the Series, but lost 5–4 after giving up four runs in seven innings. The Braves ended the Series in Game 6. Greg's dream of winning a World Series had come true!

Greg and his teammates stormed the field as soon as the Indians' final out was recorded. The Braves jumped on each other and hugged each other. Afterward, the players sprayed victory champagne all over the locker room. Many of the players celebrated during the offseason by taking vacations. Greg was content to relax with Kathy and Amanda Paige, their one-year-old daughter.

The 1996 season was another strong one for Greg and the Braves. The team finished in first place with a 96–66 record. Greg posted a 2.72 ERA, walked only 28, and struck out 172. He finished with a 15–11 record but could easily have finished with 18 or 19 wins. He lost several games in which the Braves scored very few runs. In fact, the Braves scored three runs or less several times when he pitched. Teammate John Smoltz was fantastic, winning 23 games and the Cy Young Award.

The Braves faced the Dodgers in the opening round of the National League playoffs. In Game 2, Greg dismantled the Dodgers 3–2 for an impressive win. The Braves won that series in three games.

Their next opponent, the St. Louis Cardinals, proved much tougher. After Atlanta won the first game behind the strong pitching of Smoltz, Greg was set to go in Game 2. But the Cardinals were ready. They pounded Greg. Gary Gaetti belted a bases-loaded home run in the seventh-inning off Greg and the

Cards won 8–3. Even worse for the Braves, the victory sparked the Cards to win the next three games.

With St. Louis leading three games to one, the Atlanta Braves pitchers rallied and came through! After Smoltz won his second game of the series, Greg redeemed himself by combining with reliever Mark Wohlers on a six-hitter, 3–1. The Braves then won the seventh game and headed to the World Series again.

Their opponents were the tough and gritty New York Yankees. The Braves made easy work, 12–1, of the Yanks in Game 1 behind Smoltz's pitching. Greg then pitched a commanding eight innings in Game 2. He allowed six hits and walked none as the Braves won 4–0. Only 20 of the 82 pitches Greg threw were called balls. He threw three balls to only one batter as he mixed speeds and painted the corners all night.

"Maddux makes pitches look like strikes, and when you are going to swing at it, it's not," said Yankees third baseman Wade Boggs after the game. "He's a magician, the David Copperfield of pitchers."

The Series moved to Atlanta for the next three games. The Braves were excited at the idea of winning the World Series at home, in front of their fans.

The Yankees won Game 3, thanks to the clutch pitching of David Cone. They surprised the Braves again in Game 4 with Jim Leyritz's late-inning hitting. Then Yankee ace Andy Pettite outdueled Smoltz 1–0 as the Yankees won all three games in Atlanta.

Greg is an excellent pitcher, but even he has a bad game sometimes.

Greg pitched Game 6, back in New York. He faltered just once, in the third inning. Greg was throwing too high in the strike zone, and the Yankee batters jumped all over him. Paul O'Neill led off the inning with a double. Joe Girardi banged a triple, deep to left-centerfield, and then Derek Jeter and Bernie Williams each drove in runs with singles. Greg pitched magnificently for the rest of the game, but it was too late. The Braves could only muster two runs and lost 3–2. The Yankees were the champions.

Greg didn't let himself get too discouraged, even in defeat. He had pitched yet another outstanding season and his powerhouse Atlanta Braves were sure to be contenders again for years to come. Greg has already written his place in baseball history as one of its best pitchers. And he is far from done writing his story.

Career Highlights

Minor League Statistics

Year	Team	League	Record	Games	Innings pitched	Hits	Runs	Earned Runs	Home Runs	Walks	Strike outs	ERA
1984	Pikeville	Rookie	6–2	14	85.2	63	35	25	2	41	62	2.63
1985	Peori	A	13–9	27	186.0	176	86	66	9	52	125	3.19
1986	Pittsfield	AA	4–3	8	63.2	49	22	19	1	15	35	2.69
1986	Iowa	AAA	10–1	18	128.1	127	49	43	3	30	65	3.02
1987	Iowa	AAA	3–0	4	27.2	17	3	3	1	12	22	0.98
	Totals		36–15	71	491.1	432	195	156	16	150	309	2.86

Major League Statistics

Year	Team	League	Record	Games	Innings pitched	Hits	Runs	Earned Runs	Home Runs	Walks	Strike outs	ERA
1986	Chicago	National	2–4	6	31.0	44	20	19	3	11	20	5.52
1987	Chicago	National	6–14	30	155.2	181	111	97	17	74	101	5.61
1988	Chicago	National	18–8	34	249.0	230	97	88	13	81	140	3.18
1989	Chicago	National	19–12	35	238.1	222	90	78	13	82	135	2.95
1990	Chicago	National	15–15	35	237.0	242	116	91	11	71	144	3.46
1991	Chicago	National	15–11	37	263.0	232	113	98	18	66	198	3.35
1992	Chicago	National	20–11	35	268.0	201	68	65	7	70	199	2.18
1993	Atlanta	National	20–10	36	267.0	228	85	70	14	52	197	2.36
1994	Atlanta	National	16–6	25	202.0	150	44	35	4	31	156	1.56
1995	Atlanta	National	19–2	28	209.2	147	39	38	8	23	181	1.63
1996	Atlanta	National	15–11	35	245.0	225	85	74	11	28	172	2.72
	Totals		165–104	336	2,365.2	2,102	868	753	119	589	1,643	2.86

Honors
- Awarded National League Gold Glove, 1990–96
- Named National League Cy Young Award winner, 1992–95
- Named National League Pitcher of the Year, 1993–95

Glossary

at bat: An official attempt to hit a pitched ball. Hitting a sacrifice, being walked, or being hit by a pitch don't count as an at bat.

changeup: A pitch that is thrown with the same motion as a fastball but with much less force, so that it travels more slowly than the batter expects.

count: The number of balls and strikes against a batter. The number of balls is always given first. For example, if the umpire has called two strikes on the batter but Greg has also thrown three balls to him, the count is 3-and-2 (three balls and two strikes).

curveball: A pitch that is thrown so it spins downward and to the right or left of the batter.

cut fastball: A type of fastball that spins downward.

earned run average (ERA): The average number of earned runs a pitcher gives up per game. An earned run is a run that scores without the help of an error by the fielding team. To calculate a pitcher's ERA, divide the total number of earned runs scored against him or her by the total number of innings pitched. Then multiply that number by nine.

free agent: A player who does not have a contract with any team.

letter of intent: A letter in which a high school student-athlete says which college he or she plans to attend.

offspeed pitching: Throwing the ball slower than usual, or slower than the batter expects.

painted the corners: When the pitcher throws the ball so that it just barely crosses a corner of home plate, he or she is said to have "painted the corners."

pinch runner: A player who is sent into the game to run for a player who has reached base.

pitching mechanics: A pitcher's windup and delivery.

short-hopped: A batted ball that bounces unexpectedly close to the fielder.

slider: A pitch that curves like a curveball but not as much.

Sources

Information for this book was obtained from the following sources: The Associated Press, 4 November 1993, 25 October 1994; Rod Beaton (*USA Today*, 18 July 1988); Ben Brown (*USA Today*, 1 August 1995); Gerry Callahan (*Sports Illustrated*, 28 October 1996); George Castle (*Sport*, May 1993); Murray Chass (*The New York Times*, 4 March 1996, 27 October 1996, 22 October 1996, 22 October 1995); Dan Dieffenbach (*Sport*, January 1995); John Giannone (*New York Post*, 29 July 1994); Jerome Holtzman (*Chicago Tribune*, 19 August 1990); Frank Isola (*New York Post*, 11 December 1992); Chuck Johnson (*USA Today*, 25 October 1994); Curry Kirkpatrick (*Newsweek*, 9 October 1995); Bob Klapisch (*Daily News* (New York), 18 August 1988, 28 October 1996); Tim Kurkjian (*Sports Illustrated*, 4 July 1994); Peter Pascarelli (*The Sporting News*, 11 July 1988); Steve Rushin (*Sports Illustrated*, 5 April 1993); Bob Verdi (*The Sporting News*, 30 November 1992); Tom Verducci (*Sports Illustrated*, 14 August 1995); George Willis (*The New York Times*, 17 October 1996, 11 October 1996).

Index

Write to Greg:

You can send mail to Greg at the address on the right. If you write a letter, don't get your hopes up too high. Greg and other athletes get lots of letters every day, and they aren't always able to answer them all.

Greg Maddux
c/o The Atlanta Braves
P.O. Box 4064
Atlanta, GA 30302

Acknowledgments

Photographs are reproduced with the permission of: © John Klein: pp. 1, 58; © Mickey Pfleger/Sports California: pp. 2, 14; Sports-Chrome East/West, Rob Tringali Jr.: pp. 6, 29; Reuters/Joe Hammer/Archive Photos: p. 9; National Baseball Library and Archive, Cooperstown, N.Y.: pp. 11, 42; Reuters/Colin Braley/Archive Photos: p. 12; AP/Wide World Photos: pp. 15, 30, 32, 35, 39, 43, 49, 53, 54; Valley High School, Las Vegas, Nevada: pp. 16, 20, 23; Bob McDonough, Berkshire Eagle: pp. 24, 27; SportsChrome East/West: p. 36; Reuters/Ray Stubblebine/Archive Photos: p. 40; Reuters/John Kuntz/Archive Photos: p. 45; Reuters/Marc Pesetsky/Archive Photos: p. 46; © ALL-SPORT USA/Jed Jacobsohn: p. 50; Reuters/Mike Blake/Archive Photos: p. 57.

Front cover photograph by SportsChrome East/West, Michael Zito. Back cover photograph by AP/Wide World Photos. Artwork by John Erste.

About the Author

John A. Torres is the author of three other sports biographies for young readers. A freelance writer, John lives with his family in New York.